# UROMASTYX AS HOME PETS

Everything You Need To Know About Uromastyx Keeping, Breeding, Housing, Feeding And Nutrition, Health Care, Conversation, Habitat And Why They Make Great Pets.

BY

**RAPH FRANCIS**

# <u>TABLE OF CONTENTS</u>

### <u>*CHAPTER 1:*</u>

UROMASTYX INTRODUCTION

### <u>*CHAPTER 2:*</u>

SELECTING THE APPROPRIATE UROMASTYX SPECIES

### <u>*CHAPTER 3:*</u>

CREATING THE IDEAL ENVIRONMENT

### <u>*CHAPTER 4:*</u>

DIET AND NUTRITION

**<u>*CHAPTER 10:*</u>**

UROMASTYX MAINTENANCE AND CARE

**<u>*CHAPTER 11:*</u>**

UROMASTYX OWNERSHIP: ETHICAL CONSIDERATIONS

**<u>*CHAPTER 12:*</u>**

TAKING PLEASURE IN UROMASTYX: SOCIAL AND CULTURAL ACTIVITIES

**<u>*CHAPTER 13:*</u>**

FREQUENTLY ASKED QUESTION AND ANSWERS (FAQS)

## *CHAPTER 1:*

# UROMASTYX INTRODUCTION

A remarkable group of reptiles found in arid areas of Africa, the Middle East, and portions of Asia are called uromastyx, or spiny-tailed lizards. Due to their distinctive features and very minimal maintenance care needs when compared to other reptiles, Uromastyx, which are well-known for their resilient temperament, distinctive spiny tails, and herbivorous diet, are becoming more and more popular as pets. The fundamentals of Uromastyx, their natural habitats, the history of domestication, and the reasons they make wonderful pets will all be covered in this chapter.

### Uromastyx Species Overview

Uromastyx are members of the Agamidae family and are distinguished by their thick bodies, strong, spiky tails, and a variety of colors and sizes, depending on the species. Although juvenile Uromastyx may consume insects in their early life stages, they are mostly herbivorous lizards. The little and bright Uromastyx ornata, which is well-known for its vivid hues, to the bigger Uromastyx aegyptia, which can reach a length of 76 centimeters (30 inches), are among the several species of Uromastyx.

Uromastyx are endemic to desert regions, where they have adapted to harsh weather and high temperatures. They are mostly diurnal, which means they are active during the day, and they have a reputation for controlling their body temperature by tanning in the sun. In addition to being a distinctive characteristic, their spiky tails act as a protection measure to ward off predators in the environment.

### Natural Environment and Conduct

In their native environment, Uromastyx lizards inhabit rocky terrains and deserts, where they reside in tunnels to avoid the severe heat of the day and the freezing nights. Additionally, these burrows provide defense against predators. Being very territorial, uromastyx often defend their burrows with great vigor against other lizards or outsiders. This territorial behavior in captivity might show itself as a desire for plenty of space, therefore it's critical for owners to build a spacious cage that fits their needs.

Uromastyx are mostly herbivores in the wild, consuming a variety of desert plants, such as leaves, flowers, and seeds. Their diet makes sense for their desert habitat, where there is little water and they have evolved to take moisture from their food. Since Uromastyx are excellent water savers, they don't need a water dish in their cage like many other reptiles do. Fresh, leafy greens, on the other hand, guarantee that animals kept in confinement stay well hydrated.

### *The Domestication of Uromastyx in History*

Due to their unique appearance and tendency to live in deserts, uromastyx have been known about and researched for ages, but as pets, they are relatively new. In the past, the majority of observations of Uromastyx were made in the wild, or they were collected and used for food or traditional medicine in some societies. Nonetheless, due in large part to the growing interest of hobbyists and reptile lovers in their distinctive qualities, uromastyx have become increasingly accessible in the pet trade in recent decades.

Comparing Uromastyx to other reptiles like geckos or snakes, domesticating them as pets is still relatively new. However, uromastyx are becoming a more popular option for reptile owners due to the growth of ethical breeding programs and a greater awareness of their care requirements. For those seeking a low-maintenance and eye-catching reptile, they are a compelling choice due to their resilient nature, herbivorous diet, and captivating demeanor.

### *Reasons Uromastyx Are Excellent Pets*

Uromastyx have gained popularity among reptile lovers for a number of reasons. First and foremost, since they eat only plants—fresh fruits, veggies, and seeds are easily obtained in most grocery stores—their herbivorous diet makes upkeep extremely simple. Uromastyx are carnivorous reptiles that need sophisticated diets or live food to survive, however they do well on basic plant-based diets.

Apart from their food, Uromastyx are renowned for their submissive nature. Raised in captivity, they are normally placid and simple to handle, however they may be territorial with other Uromastyx. For those who are unfamiliar with reptiles or are searching for a low-stress companion, this makes them an excellent choice.

In addition, Uromastyx are long-term companions since they often live 15 to 20 years or more in captivity with the right care.

They are also visually attractive because of their distinctive look, which includes vivid colors and prominent tails. Depending on the species and age of the lizard, several Uromastyx species display amazing color changes, ranging from vivid yellows and oranges to deep blues and greens. Because of their remarkable coloring, robust nature, and captivating activity, Uromastyx are now a well-liked option for reptile pets.

<u>*CHAPTER 2:*</u>

# SELECTING THE APPROPRIATE UROMASTYX SPECIES

One of the most important choices you will have to make as a prospective Uromastyx owner is selecting the appropriate species. The process of choosing the best species for your house may be difficult since there are over 15 recognized species, each with distinct physical traits, mannerisms, and maintenance needs. An extensive overview of the several species of Uromastyx, their salient characteristics, and the variables to take into account when selecting the most suitable one for your skill level and lifestyle will be given in this chapter.

### *Uromastyx Species Overview*

The size, color, and environmental requirements of uromastyx species vary greatly, so it's important to do your homework on the particular species you're thinking about. Following are a few of the most popular animals maintained as pets:

***1. Mali Uromastyx, or Uromastyx maliensis*** – Mali Uromastyx, one of the most well-liked species kept in captivity, are distinguished by their remarkable black and yellow coloring and relatively tiny stature (they may reach up to 15 inches). They are a fantastic option for novice reptile owners since they are versatile and comparatively robust.

**2. Ornate Uromastyx, or Uromastyx ornata –** This species is highly valued for its vivid coloring, which often displays orange, blue, and green tones. Because of their somewhat more sensitive care needs, ornate uromastyx could be better suited for keepers with greater expertise.

**3. Egyptian Uromastyx, or Uromastyx aegyptia** – Egyptian Uromastyx is the biggest species of Uromastyx, reaching a maximum length of 30 inches. Larger cages and more specialized environmental conditions are necessary for these reptiles because of their size, which makes them better suited for experienced reptile keepers.

**4. Saharan Uromastyx, Uromastyx geyri –** Medium-sized and generally simple to care for in captivity, Saharan Uromastyx are distinguished by their vivid red or orange colors. They are a well-liked option for anyone seeking a manageable species with vibrant colors.

**5.** ***Moroccan Uromastyx, Uromastyx acanthinura*** – With a maximum length of 18 inches, these medium-sized lizards are rather calm and tolerant of being kept in captivity. They have an eye-catching reddish-brown coloring with vibrant highlights.

***Important Features to Take Into Account***

There are a few things to think about while selecting an Uromastyx species that may affect your ownership experience:

***1. Size:*** The Ornate Uromastyx, which is smaller and measures around 10 to 14 inches, is significantly smaller than the Egyptian

Uromastyx, which may reach a height of 30 inches. The size of the species will influence the level of care required as well as the amount of cage area required. Greater room, more powerful heating sources, and heavier cages are needed for larger species.

**2. *Temperament:*** Although the majority of Uromastyx are calm and peaceful, certain species are more prone to aggressive behavior or stress than others. For instance, compared to the tranquil and laid-back Mali Uromastyx, the Ornate Uromastyx could be more reticent. You can decide whether a lizard will fit well with your home setting by learning about each species' disposition.

**3. *colors:*** The vivid and diverse colors of Uromastyx is one of their primary attractions.

While some species, like the Saharan Uromastyx, display flaming reds and oranges, others, like the Ornate Uromastyx, are distinguished by their bright blues and greens. The lizards are even more intriguing to watch since their color may change based on their emotions or body temperature.

**4. *Environmental Needs:*** Because Uromastyx species are distributed over the globe, their environmental needs might differ. Certain species—like the Egyptian Uromastyx—need greater dryness and higher temperatures, while other species could be more tolerant of a wider range of circumstances. When selecting a species, it is crucial to take into account the temperature and surroundings that you may create in your house.

### *Elements to Take Into Account While Choosing an Uromastyx*

It is important to consider your personal skill level as well as the time and effort you are prepared to commit to the maintenance of your chosen Uromastyx species. A species like the Mali Uromastyx, which is renowned for its versatility and resilience, would be a good choice for novice reptile keepers to begin with. For those seeking a greater challenge or more experience, a species like the Egyptian Uromastyx, which needs a bigger, more specialized environment, would be a good choice.

Take into account the species' accessibility in your region as well. While certain Uromastyx species are simpler to locate and are more often raised in captivity, others could be harder to find. Buying from a reliable breeder or rescue group is the best way to guarantee that your Uromastyx has been reared

***In good health and is unaffected by illness.***

Lastly, consider the increased time commitment required for maintaining an Uromastyx. These lizards have a maximum lifespan of 15 to 20 years when given the right care. Before you make your ultimate choice, be sure you are ready to take on the responsibilities of taking care of a long-lived reptile.

You may choose an Uromastyx species that will flourish in your house and provide you years of intrigue and friendship by carefully weighing these criteria.

## *CHAPTER 3:*

# CREATING THE IDEAL ENVIRONMENT

For the sake of an Uromastyx's health and welfare, the ideal environment must be created. It is essential to replicate these circumstances in captivity since these desert-dwelling reptiles have evolved to survive in hard, dry settings with high temperatures and little humidity. In addition to being comfortable, a well-designed environment encourages your Uromastyx to engage in healthy activities like hiding, digging, and basking—all of which are critical for their mental and physical well-being. This chapter will cover the many components that go into creating the ideal Uromastyx habitat, such as substrate, lighting, humidity, warmth, and enclosure type and size.

## *Sizes and Types of Enclosures*

Selecting the ideal cage is the first step in creating a home for your Uromastyx. Your lizard should be able to walk about, bathe, and explore the cage, but it should also have enough room for hiding places and safe locations. The kind of Uromastyx you have will determine how big the enclosure has to be; bigger species, like the Egyptian Uromastyx, will need a lot more room than smaller species, like the Ornate Uromastyx.

A minimum enclosure size of 4 feet long by 2 feet wide is advised for smaller species, while an enclosure as big as 6 feet long by 3 feet wide may be necessary for larger species. Since Uromastyx are terrestrial lizards and do not need a lot of vertical space, height is not as important. To allow for appropriate heat and UVB lamp positioning, it is typically advised to have a minimum height of two feet.

Because glass terrariums are transparent and need little upkeep, they are a common option for Uromastyx cages. Nonetheless, front-opening doors made of wood or PVC may also work well as they provide superior insulation and can sustain the high temperatures needed for Uromastyx. Make that the enclosure has enough ventilation to avoid heat accumulation and to facilitate appropriate air circulation, regardless of the material used.

### *Lighting and Heating*

Keeping the right temperature gradient in place is one of the most crucial elements of an Uromastyx environment. Since uromastyx are ectothermic, their body temperature is controlled by outside heat sources. They need the daytime sun to warm up in the wild, so it's critical to mimic this habit in captivity by creating a warm space for them to bask in.

Maintaining the basking area at a temperature between 120°F and 130°F (49°C and 54°C) can help to replicate the intense heat seen in their native habitat. This may be accomplished by placing a ceramic heat emitter or a high-wattage basking light atop a specially marked basking rock or platform. To enable your Uromastyx to thermoregulate—moving between warmer and colder sections as needed—the remaining portion of the cage should contain a cooler section with temperatures between 85°F and 95°F (29°C and 35°C). Temperatures may dip to between 70°F and 75°F (21°C and 24°C) at night without endangering your lizard.

Uromastyx needs heat and UVB radiation in order to generate vitamin D3, which is necessary for healthy bones and calcium absorption. To give the cage 10 to 12 hours of light each day, a UVB lamp has to be installed. Even while the UVB bulb continues to generate visible light, its efficacy decreases with time, so be sure to change it every six to twelve months.

***Humidity Management***

Uromastyx are desert-dwelling reptiles that have evolved to survive in conditions with very little humidity. Replicating these circumstances in captivity requires maintaining an enclosure humidity of less than 40%. It's critical to routinely check the humidity in the enclosure of your Uromastyx since high humidity levels may cause skin infections, breathing difficulties, and other health concerns.

Refrain from utilizing water features or misting the enclosure if you want to maintain low humidity. Fresh veggies and leafy greens, on the other hand, have moisture that your Uromastyx can remove, so use them to hydrate instead. A small water dish may be provided sometimes, if needed, but it should be taken out a few hours later to avoid increasing the enclosure's humidity levels.

Controlling humidity requires proper ventilation, so make sure there is enough airflow and proper ventilation inside the enclosure. You may need to use a dehumidifier in the area where the enclosure is stored to maintain the right levels if you live in a very humid region.

### *Options for Substrate*

The bedding, or substrate, of your uromastyx's cage is crucial for simulating their native habitat and encouraging burrowing and other natural habits. There are several substrate alternatives available; nevertheless, it is crucial to choose one that is simple to clean, pleasant, and safe.

Sand and dirt or sand and clay combinations are excellent substrate choices for Uromastyx because they closely resemble the natural desert ecosystem. This kind of ground promotes low humidity levels while enabling burrowing and digging. Play sand may be mixed with clay or organic topsoil in a 3:1 ratio to make a substrate mix. In order to facilitate digging, the substrate should be between two and four inches deep. If your Uromastyx so desires, there should be a deeper region in one corner for burrowing.

Using reptile carpet or tile as a substrate is an additional choice. They are not susceptible to impaction, which may happen if your Uromastyx inadvertently consumes loose substrate, and they are very simple to clean. They do not, however, provide the same potential for burrowing or digging, so you may need to offer other enrichment, such as pebbles or hides.

Substrates such as wood chips, coconut fiber, or calcium sand should not be used since they may impact if consumed or make the atmosphere excessively humid for Uromastyx.

## *Accents & Decorations*

In order to provide your Uromastyx a stimulating habitat, it's vital to decorate the enclosure with pebbles, hides, and other enrichment materials. Your Uromastyx may absorb heat by basking in a warm region created by placing large, flat pebbles underneath the basking light. Uromastyx may be rather busy, so make sure these pebbles are sturdy and won't fall or move. You don't want to unintentionally disturb them.

Finding hiding places is also crucial to giving your Uromastyx a feeling of security. Hollow logs, commercially supplied reptile skins, or hides made from slate or pebbles may all be used. To provide your Uromastyx the opportunity to hide in various temperature ranges, make sure the hides are positioned in both the warm and cold sections of the enclosure.

To promote exploration and movement, you may also give climbing branches, platforms, or other enrichment materials. Although uromastyx are mostly ground-dwelling reptiles, they sometimes like climbing rocks or logs to study or enjoy their surroundings.

**Upkeep and Cleaning**

The cleanliness of the cage is critical to your Uromastyx's health and wellbeing. Frequent enclosure cleaning will lower the risk of sickness by preventing the growth of germs and eliminating excrement, uneaten food, and contaminated substrate. Every few weeks, the cage has to be thoroughly cleaned, with the substrate replaced, all surfaces sanitized, and all décor and hides cleaned.

Any dangerous germs or parasites may be eliminated by using a suitable disinfectant for reptiles or a diluted bleach solution (1 part bleach to 10 parts water). When reintroducing your Uromastyx, make sure you rinse the cage well to get rid of any residue and let it dry fully.

By following these suggestions for setting up and maintaining your Uromastyx's habitat, you can create a secure, comfortable, and stimulating environment that supports their health and well-being in captivity.

## *CHAPTER 4:*

# DIET AND NUTRITION

The diet of Uromastyx is exclusively herbivorous, consisting mostly of leafy greens, vegetables, seeds, and flowers, making them unusual among reptiles. The easy-to-find and prepared plant-based meals that Uromastyx like to eat are in contrast to the diets of many other lizards, which call for live insects or small mammals. However, feeding the appropriate combination of nutrients is vital to promote the long-term health and well-being of your Uromastyx. The dietary requirements of Uromastyx will be covered in this chapter, along with their favorite meals, feeding regimens, and crucial nutritional factors.

### *Essentials of a Herbivorous Diet*

In the wild, grasses, leaves, flowers, seeds, and sometimes fruits are among the many plant-based meals that Uromastyx lizards search for. In settings where water is limited, they have evolved to absorb moisture and nutrients from their diet, and their highly specialized digestive systems are designed to handle tough plant material. For their health to be maintained in captivity, this diet must be replicated.

Rich in fiber, vitamins, and minerals, leafy greens should be the cornerstone of any Uromastyx diet. Collard greens, mustard greens, turnip greens, dandelion greens, and escarole are some of the greatest greens available. Calcium and vitamin A, which are crucial for strong bones, a healthy immune system, and general vigor, are included in these greens.

To add variation to your Uromastyx's diet, you should provide a range of vegetables in addition to leafy greens. Carrots, bell peppers, zucchini, and squash are all great choices. With a balanced diet, these veggies help keep your Uromastyx busy and provide extra vitamins and minerals. Be careful to slice veggies into tiny, manageable pieces to make them simpler for your lizard to consume.

Small portions of fruits, such as figs, papaya, or berries, may be given sometimes as treats, but because of their high sugar content, fruits should only be supplied in moderation. Consuming too much fruit might result in restricting them to once or twice a month to avoid weight or digestive problems.

## *Blossoms and Seeds*

A Uromastyx's diet also includes seeds and blossoms, which are significant sources of extra fiber and minerals. In the wild, Uromastyx often eat the seeds of dry desert plants; you may mimic this behavior in your captive bird by providing modest quantities of millet, chia, or bird seed mixtures. Given their high fat content and potential to cause weight gain if overfed, seeds should only be administered in small amounts.

Your Uromastyx may benefit from eating edible flowers as well, such as hibiscus, dandelion blooms, and nasturtiums. These flowers may be an enrichment source since Uromastyx often like browsing and nibbling on flowers. They are also rich in vitamins. Make sure the flowers you provide are devoid of chemicals or pesticides, and steer clear of any blooms that might be harmful to reptiles.

## Vitamin and Calcium Supplements

As calcium is crucial for bone health, muscular function, and general development, feeding Uromastyx the right amount is one of the most crucial parts of their diet. Although leafy greens like collards and dandelions are naturally rich in calcium, metabolic bone disease, a prevalent ailment in reptiles caused by calcium insufficiency, may be avoided by taking supplemental calcium supplements.

At least twice or three times a week, you may give your Uromastyx calcium by sprinkling its diet with a powder made specifically for reptiles. If UVB illumination is inadequate for your Uromastyx, make sure the calcium supplement you choose includes vitamin D3. This is because calcium absorption depends on this vitamin. But use caution when taking excessive amounts of vitamin D3 since this may be hazardous.

To complement any vitamins and minerals that they may not be getting enough of in their diet, a multivitamin supplement should be given once or twice a week. By doing this, you can make sure that your Uromastyx eats a balanced, well-rounded diet that promotes their general health.

***Feeding Timetable and Amounts***

Feeding uromastyx on a daily basis is recommended, with portions according to their size and degree of activity. Due to their increased nutritional demands and quick growth, younger Uromastyx may need bigger quantities and more frequent feedings. Your Uromastyx's metabolism will slow down as they become older and they may not need as much food.

Offering enough food to cover a shallow dish or a rock's flat surface is a basic rule of thumb. After a few hours, remove any food that hasn't been eaten to avoid spoiling it. Since uromastyx are often busy throughout the day, feeding them in the morning will enable them to enjoy and process their food throughout the day.

Though Uromastyx often get the majority of their hydration from the moisture in their meal, make sure that fresh water is constantly accessible. While some keepers choose to softly sprinkle their food to enhance moisture, others decide to give a little water dish. Water dishes may raise the humidity in an enclosure in dry conditions, so keep that in mind and take the dish out if needed.

### Steer clear of harmful foods

Not every fruit, vegetable, or leafy green is healthy for Uromastyx, therefore it's crucial to keep them away from potentially dangerous items. High concentrations of oxalates are found in several greens, including spinach, kale, and chard. These compounds may bind to calcium and inhibit its absorption. These need to be consumed in moderation or not at all.

Your Uromastyx shouldn't regularly eat iceberg lettuce and other pale lettuce since they are low in nutrients. Furthermore, stay away from giving your Uromastyx foods rich in phosphorus, since this may cause metabolic bone disease and interfere with the absorption of calcium.

Avoiding processed meals, sugary snacks, and high-fat foods is also advised since they may contribute to liver disease, obesity, and other health problems. Replicate as much as you can the natural diet of your Uromastyx by sticking to natural, plant-based meals.

**Monitoring Food Requirements and Health**

In order to make sure your Uromastyx is getting enough food and staying at a healthy weight, you need to keep an eye on their feeding patterns. A healthy Uromastyx should not seem overweight or bloated, but rather have a rounded body with a significant fat storage near the base of the tail. A persistent refusal to eat or weight loss in your Uromastyx may indicate a medical problem, stress, or unfavorable environmental circumstances.

On the other hand, you may need to decrease the frequency of goodies like fruits or seeds or modify the portion sizes if your Uromastyx is starting to gain weight. You may detect any changes in your Uromastyx's health early on and make the required dietary modifications by regularly weighing them and monitoring their weight.

## *Final Thoughts*

Providing your Uromastyx with a plant-based, well-balanced diet is essential to its lifespan and overall health. You can make sure your Uromastyx gets all the nutrients they need to flourish by providing a range of leafy greens, veggies, seeds, and flowers in addition to the required supplements. You can maintain a happy and healthy Uromastyx under your care by keeping a regular eye on their food patterns and making modifications as necessary.

## *CHAPTER 5:*

# UROMASTYX HOUSING AND ENVIRONMENTAL SETUP

The proper housing and environmental setup are essential for the wellbeing of Uromastyx when kept as pets. In the wild, Uromastyx live in dry desert areas where they hide underground and enjoy the sun. Maintaining these natural environments in captivity can help keep your Uromastyx happy, active, and healthy. The key elements of designing the perfect home for your Uromastyx are covered in this chapter, along

with information on enclosure size, substrate, lighting, heating, and accessories.

### *Size and Type of Enclosure*

The size of the cage should be your first priority when building up your Uromastyx's home. Because uromastyx are busy lizards, they need plenty of room to roam, sunbathe, and investigate. A minimum cage size of 4 feet long by 2 feet wide is advised for mature Uromastyx, while bigger enclosures are usually preferable. A 3-foot-long cage could work for smaller species or youngsters, but as they become bigger, you'll need to improve their habitat to provide them additional room.

For Uromastyx, glass terrariums or specially constructed wooden enclosures with front-opening doors are often used. While wooden or PVC enclosures provide superior insulation—which is crucial for preserving the high temperatures that Uromastyx require—glass enclosures allow for better sight. It doesn't matter what kind of cage you select—Uromastyx are inquisitive and powerful climbers—as long as it has doors or a tight cover to keep them out.

### *Selection of Substrate*

Creating a cozy and organic habitat for your Uromastyx depends largely on the substrate you choose. Since Uromastyx are found in rocky or sandy settings in nature, it's critical to choose a substrate that closely resembles this environment. There are several substrate choices, each with advantages and disadvantages:

*1. Play Sand:* Because it closely mimics their native desert habitat, fine, clean play sand is a popular option for Uromastyx cages. In addition to being simple to spot-clean, it allows Uromastyx to burrow, something they like doing. However, if consumed, sand may cause impaction, so watch your Uromastyx's behavior and don't use it on little or very young people.

*2. Soil-Sand Mix:* Compared to pure sand, a combination of soil and sand may provide a more realistic ground that is more suited for holding burrows. Better humidity management is another benefit of this approach, which is beneficial in arid conditions. Make sure the soil you choose is suitable for reptiles and devoid of chemicals.

*3. Reptile Carpeting:* Reptile carpeting is an easier-to-maintain, cleaner alternative to loose surfaces for individuals who desire it. It lessens the chance of impaction and is machine washable. It does not, however, permit digging, which can restrict the normal activity of your Uromastyx.

*4. Tile or Slate:* Some custodians use slate or flat tiles for their substrate. These materials provide a stable surface for sunbathing and are simple to clean. By placing loose sand in certain spots, you may provide the best of both worlds for your Uromastyx burrowing conditions.

### Heating and Controlling Temperature

Uromastyx are ectothermic reptiles, meaning they depend on external heat sources to control their body temperature. In the wild, they take refuge in burrows or other shaded spots to cool down after basking in the sun. You must establish a temperature gradient in the cage, with a warmer side for basking and a colder side, in order to duplicate this.

The enclosure's warmest spot should be the basking area, where temperatures may get to between 110°F and 130°F. This may be accomplished by placing a ceramic heat emitter or a high-wattage basking lamp immediately over a basking surface, such as slate or flat rock. It's crucial to place the heat source so that your Uromastyx can warm up effectively by basking directly beneath it.

During the day, the temperature on the cooler side of the enclosure should be between 85°F and 90°F. Your Uromastyx may adjust its body temperature by moving between warmer and colder regions as required thanks to this temperature gradient. Temperatures may dip to between 70°F and 75°F at night since Uromastyx are used to colder desert evenings.

## *UVB Illumination*

Uromastyx need heat and ultraviolet B (UVB) light exposure in order to generate vitamin D3, which is necessary for healthy bones and the absorption of calcium. In the absence of sufficient UVB illumination, Uromastyx are susceptible to metabolic bone disease, a dangerous ailment that may result in weakness and abnormalities.

To simulate natural sunshine, install UVB lamps above the basking area and leave them on for 10 to 12 hours every day. Even though the bulbs are still emitting visible light, it is recommended that they be changed every six to twelve months due to a gradual decline in their UVB output.

On warm days, you can also give your Uromastyx access to natural sunshine by bringing it outdoors for supervised bouts of basking. you prevent overheating, be sure you provide shade and keep an eye on the temperature.

### *Hydration and Humidity*

Since uromastyx are evolved to dry climates, their cage should have low humidity levels, ideally between 20% and 30%. It's critical to keep an eye on humidity levels and make sure the enclosure has enough ventilation since high humidity may cause respiratory infections and other health problems.

Even though the moisture in their food provides Uromastyx with most of their hydration, it's still a good idea to include a small water dish in the cage. Some Uromastyx may take a sip from it, while others would just brush it off. If you live in a humid region, be sure to remove the dish if it increases the humidity levels too high. You should also replace the water often to avoid bacterial development.

***Accessories and Enrichment for Enclosures***

Adding a range of gadgets and hiding places to your Uromastyx's cage will help to create a habitat that is both interesting and enriching for them. Branches, slate, and flat rocks may be utilized to provide places for sunbathing and climbing. Since uromastyx like to burrow, you may provide them with a safe haven in the form of artificial tunnels constructed of PVC pipes or cork bark, or a deep substrate layer.

Since hiding places make your Uromastyx feel secure and shielded, they are crucial for lowering stress levels. Reptile skins that are sold commercially may be used, or you can make your own out of clay pots, wood, and pebbles. Make sure the enclosure has plenty of hiding places for your Uromastyx, both in the warm and cold sections, so they may select their favorite position.

**Upkeep and Cleaning**

Enclosure cleanliness and hygienic conditions are critical to the well-being of your uromastyx. Every day, remove any uneaten food, waste, and trash from the enclosure. Do a thorough cleaning once a month by washing the accessories, disinfecting the surfaces, and renewing the substrate. Use disinfectants specifically designed for reptiles; strong chemicals may be detrimental to your Uromastyx.

### Final Thoughts

For the sake of your Uromastyx's health and wellbeing, you must set up their habitat and home properly. You can make sure that your Uromastyx survives in captivity by giving it a roomy habitat, the right substrate, warmth, UVB illumination, and enrichment. In addition to preventing health problems, regular cleaning and upkeep will provide your pet a cozy and fascinating environment.

## *CHAPTER 6:*

# TAKING CARE OF AND GETTING ALONG WITH YOUR UROMASTYX

Uromastyx are renowned for being independent and reticent, but with the right care and socialization, they may grow to love engagement and even feel more at ease with their owners. Although uromastyx are not usually amiable pets, they may develop strong ties with their owners and show inquisitive and gregarious tendencies when they feel secure. The best ways to handle, socialize, and establish trust with your Uromastyx are covered in this chapter, so you may have a great experience with your pet as well.

### *Comprehending Uromastyx Conduct*

It's critical to comprehend your Uromastyx Is innate temperament and behavior before you start training them. Animals classified as uromastyx are often solitary and most active during the day. They spend their time in the outdoors feeding and sunbathing, and when they sense danger, they withdraw to their burrows. Uromastyx are a prey species, therefore they might be wary and need some time to adjust to their surroundings.

Uromastyx may display protective responses, such tail-whipping, body puffing, or hiding in their hide, when they are initially brought into their new environment. These actions are normal and shouldn't be seen as hostile. With time and careful handling, most Uromastyx will grow more calm and acclimated to human contact.

## Establishing Trust by Patience

Patience is the key to effectively managing and socializing your Uromastyx. Before trying to handle your Uromastyx, it's crucial to give them some time to become used to their new surroundings. To begin, observe your Uromastyx from a distance and give them time to become used to seeing you. To prevent frightening them, you might walk gently, talk quietly, and sit close to their cage.

You may start hand-feeding your Uromastyx after it seems more at ease and calm. One of the best ways to foster pleasant associations and establish trust is to provide food with your hands. Let them come to you at their own speed and use their favorite goodies, such little bits of vegetable or flower. Steer clear of abrupt movements and wait for your uromastyx to approach you when they are ready.

**Managing Methods**

**If your uromastyx is larger than**

Once they feel at ease with you, you may start interacting with them. It's crucial to approach your Uromastyx with poise and calm as any hesitancy or abrupt movements might make them afraid. Uromastyx do not like to have their tails grasped or lifted, thus they should always be supported by both hands.

Using one hand to hold their chest and belly and the other to gently move their rear legs, you may pick up your Uromastyx. As you carefully and gradually raise them, make sure they feel safe. Refrain from grasping your uromastyx too firmly, as this may lead to tension and increase the likelihood of difficulties. As soon as you get them in your hands, hold them close to your body to give yourself security.

It's crucial to remember that not every Uromastyx will take well to handling; in fact, some may feel better off staying in their cage. If your pet seems anxious or uncomfortable, don't force them to engage; instead, respect their own choices. With gradual handling and encouraging feedback, many Uromastyx will get used to being handled.

## *Interaction and Enhancement*

Apart from handling, you may socialize and maintain cerebral stimulation for your Uromastyx by offering enrichment and exploration possibilities. Because uromastyx are inherently inquisitive creatures, you may encourage them to engage more with their surroundings and with you by providing them with a range of activities and habitats.

Establishing a secure, contained space where your Uromastyx may go outside of their cage is one method to provide enrichment. For them to explore, you may put up a playpen or a safe, reptile-proofed space with tunnels, pebbles, and climbing frames. To protect your Uromastyx's safety during these sessions, always keep an eye on them, and pay attention to the lighting and temperature needs.

Providing an assortment of meals and feeding techniques is an additional means of enrichment. Since uromastyx like to forage, you may promote natural behaviors by dispersing or hiding food around their habitat. In order to pique their interest in hunting, you may also periodically provide live food, such as insects. But keep in mind that because Uromastyx are mostly herbivorous, live food should only be provided in moderation.

### Stressful Signs and How to Prevent Them

Your Uromastyx should always like being handled and socialized with. It's critical to identify stress indicators and know when to pause or modify your course of action. In Uromastyx, common indications of stress include:

*- Often hiding or withdrawing to their burrow -* Refusing food or becoming disinterested in eating - Excessive tail wagging or puffing up - *Skin tone darkening* - Panting or shallow breathing

It is crucial to allow your uromastyx some space to unwind and decrease the frequency of handling if you see any of these behaviors. Aside from sufficient lighting, warmth, and hiding places, make sure their habitat is set up properly, since environmental issues may also lead to stress.

### *Creating an Uromastyx Bond*

It takes patience and time to develop a close relationship with your Uromastyx, but the experience may be quite fulfilling. You could see your Uromastyx become more interested in you and inquisitive as they get used to being handled and interacting with you. While some Uromastyx could even come up to you in search of food or to explore, others might just like to lounge close to you.

The secret to developing a close friendship with your Uromastyx is to be consistent and give them praise. You may create a lasting connection with your pet and reap the benefits of a fulfilling relationship for years to come by giving them a secure and comfortable environment, handling them gently, and providing enrichment.

## *Final Thoughts*

Patience, compassion, and a kind attitude are necessary while handling and socializing your Uromastyx. You may create a happy and fulfilling experience for both you and your pet by learning to accept their natural behaviors and gradually earning their confidence. Keep in mind that each Uromastyx is different, and although some could want to be handled and interact with people, others might like to be left more on their own. You may have a rewarding relationship and develop a close link with your Uromastyx with patience and effort.

<u>*CHAPTER 7:*</u>

# RECOGNIZING TYPICAL UROMASTYX HEALTH CONCERNS

## *Overview of Common Health Concerns*

Like any pet, an Uromastyx lizard may have a variety of health problems, from minor to serious. Every owner of an Uromastyx must comprehend these prevalent health issues, their causes, and their solutions. This chapter will describe common health problems that these lizards may have, how to identify them, what you can do to avoid them, and when you should call a veterinarian.

### *1. MBD, or metabolic bone disease*

One of the most prevalent conditions affecting metabolic bone disease (MBD). It usually results from a calcium and vitamin D3 shortage, which weakens bones and causes a host of other health issues.

***MBD causes:*** Inadequate UVB illumination, unhealthful food choices, or a deficiency in calcium supplements are common causes of MBD. It's possible that Uromastyx won't get enough UVB exposure in captivity to make vitamin D3, which is essential for absorbing calcium.

***Symptoms of MBD:*** These may vary, but often include weakness, tiredness, lack of appetite, limb edema, and obvious bone abnormalities. In extreme circumstances, you may see that your ureomastyx is unsteady or cannot adequately support its own weight.

***Prevention and Treatment:*** Make sure your Uromastyx gets access to appropriate UVB illumination and a calcium-rich, well-balanced food in order to avoid MBD. Leafy greens and commercial supplements may be examples of this. See a veterinarian if MBD is suspected; they may suggest calcium injections or supplements, as well as changes to food and lighting.

### Infections of the Respiratory System

Uromastyx patients may be seriously at risk for respiratory infections, which are often brought on by unfavorable environmental factors like low humidity or high temperatures.

*Causes:* Respiratory infections are caused by bacteria and fungus flourishing in an environment that is too damp and inadequately heated. Additionally, handling or crowding stress might make someone more susceptible.

*Symptoms:* Common manifestations include nasal discharge, tiredness, reduced appetite, and wheezing. You may also see open-mouth breathing in your uromastyx, which is an indication of discomfort.

***Prevention and Treatment:*** Maintain appropriate humidity levels (20–40%) and make sure there's enough heating, with a basking area between 100°F and 120°F (38°C and 49°C), to avoid respiratory infections. See a veterinarian if you notice any symptoms so that you may get the proper care, which can include medications and enclosure habitat modifications.

### 3. Digestive Problems

In the Uromastyx, digestive issues including impaction might occur often. Impaction is the result of blockage in the digestive system, usually from improper substrates or dehydration.

*Causes:* Ingesting particles of the substrate, such sand or gravel, or dehydration may lead to impaction. Similar symptoms may also be caused by parasites or gastrointestinal diseases in uromastyx.

*Symptoms:* Lethargy, an appetite loss, bloating, and difficulty passing stool are indications of gastrointestinal problems. Additionally, you can see unusual feces.

*Prevention and Treatment:* Use a safe substrate (such as paper towels or ceramic tiles) and provide fresh water every day to avoid impaction. Immediately visit a veterinarian if impaction is suspected. In extreme situations, treatment may include surgery, medication, or the administration of fluids.

## 4. Insects

Both internal and external parasites may affect uromastyx. Various worms are considered internal parasites, while ticks or mites are considered exterior parasites.

***Symptoms of Parasites:*** Diarrhea, weight loss, fatigue, and skin irritation are typical indicators of parasite infections. You could sometimes also see odd behavior or excessive scratching.

***Prevention and Treatment :*** To keep an environment free of parasites, provide animals a healthy diet, and keep a distance from animals who are affected. If you suspect a parasite illness, a veterinarian may do fecal checks and propose appropriate treatments, which may include antiparasitic drugs.

### 5. Skin Problems

Inadequate humidity levels or substrate selections may lead to skin problems including infections, shedding, or scale rot.

***Symptoms:*** The skin of a healthy Uromastyx should be brightly colored, smooth, and undamaged. Open sores, redness, and irritation are some indicators of skin problems. Retained skin may also be a consequence of improper shedding, especially around the toes.

***Prevention and Treatment:*** Provide a suitable environment with the right humidity levels and substrate to avoid skin problems. See a veterinarian if you see any skin issues for a diagnosis and possible course of treatment, which may include topical or antibiotic medications.

### *Routine Health Examinations*

Regular health examinations are essential for spotting any problems early. This is how to carry out an exhaustive health assessment:

- ***Body Condition:*** Check the weight and physical state of your Uromastyx on a regular basis. A lizard that is underweight may need to have its nutrition changed.

- ***Skin and Scales:*** Examine the skin for any signs of rashes or discomfort. A healthy Uromastyx will have smooth skin and brilliant hues.

***Eyes and Mouth:*** Verify that there is no swelling or discharge and that the eyes are bright and clear. Inspect the mouth for ulcers or sores.

***Behavior:*** Keep an eye out for behavioral changes, such as lethargy or a decrease in activity, since these might point to underlying medical issues.

## *Final Thoughts*

It's crucial to comprehend and identify frequent health problems in Uromastyx lizards in order to provide the right treatment. A long, healthy life for your pet may be ensured by routine health examinations, preventive measures, and timely veterinarian care when needed. You may promote your Uromastyx's health and well-being by keeping its surroundings steady and providing proactive care.

## CHAPTER 8:

# KEEPING UROMASTYX HEALTHY AND WELL

### Overview of Wellness and Health

Your Uromastyx's general well-being depends on you taking care of its health and wellbeing. Maintaining the health of your lizard requires a multimodal strategy that involves identifying health concerns, creating a suitable habitat, making sure it eats a balanced food, and being aware of stress management. These topics will be thoroughly examined in this chapter.

## 1. Environmental Factors

Your Uromastyx needs the proper environmental conditions to be healthy. Since these lizards are endemic to dry areas, it is important to replicate such circumstances.

***Temperature:*** A temperature gradient is necessary for uromastyx in their cage. The ideal temperature range for the basking region is 100°F to 120°F (38°C to 49°C), while the colder side is 75°F to 85°F (24°C to 29°C). Use dependable thermometers to measure these temperatures routinely.

***Humidity:*** It's critical to keep humidity levels between 20% and 40% low. Infections of the respiratory system and other health issues may result from high humidity. Make sure there is enough ventilation, and don't spray too much.

***illumination:*** The health of Uromastyx depends on sufficient UVB illumination. Your lizard needs 10 to 12 hours of UVB sun exposure every day to sustain calcium metabolism. Purchase premium UVB bulbs and swap them out every six months, even if the old ones are still producing light.

***Substrate:*** Select a secure substrate that deters impaction and permits natural digging. Paper towels, ceramic tiles, and reptile carpet are safe options. Avoid loose substrates like sand that may be swallowed.

## 2. Diet

Maintaining the health of your Uromastyx requires a well-balanced diet. Knowing what they should eat may help them stay as healthy as possible and avoid health problems.

***Diet Composition:*** Uromastyx are mostly herbivores and thrive on a diet rich in leafy greens, vegetables, and certain fruits. A large amount of their diet has to consist of dark leafy greens like dandelion, mustard, and collard greens.

***Supplementation:*** You should think about giving your Uromastyx vitamin and calcium supplements to make sure they get enough nourishment. Give them a multivitamin supplement at least once a week and sprinkle some calcium supplements on their diet a couple times a week.

*Hydration:* Although Uromastyx don't need a lot of water, they still need to have access to clean water. Offer a small water dish and keep an eye on it to make sure it stays clean. Another way to aid with hydration is to spray their meals occasionally.

## 3. Routine Medical Exams

Frequent health examinations may assist in identifying any problems before they worsen. It's critical to evaluate any changes in your Uromastyx's appearance, behavior, or hunger on a weekly basis.

*Body Condition:* Keep an eye on the weight and physical state of your Uromastyx. Their bones should be palpably felt, not visibly noticeable. A lizard that is underweight may need to have its nutrition changed.

***Skin and Scales:*** Check for issues with redness, itching, or shedding on the skin. The skin of a healthy Uromastyx should be brightly colored and smooth.

***Eyes and Mouth:*** Examine for lesions, swelling, or discharge. Bright, clean eyes are indicative of good health.

***Behavioral Changes:*** Keep an eye out for any odd behavior, fatigue, or shifts in your level of activity. Early behavioral change detection may reveal underlying health problems.

## 4. Animal Health

It's crucial to build a rapport with a veterinarian who specializes in reptile care. Frequent examinations can monitor the condition of your Uromastyx and identify possible problems early.

***Selecting a Veterinarian:*** Seek a vet with expertise with Uromastyx and a focus on reptiles. During visits, talk about your lizard's food, environment, and any concerns you may have.

***Regular Check-ups:*** Regular trips to the vet may help keep your Uromastyx healthy. In addition to doing medical examinations and checking for parasites, your veterinarian may provide any required shots or treatments.

### 5. Handling Stress

For the sake of your Uromastyx Is health and wellbeing, stress management is essential. Stress may weaken someone's immune system, which can cause health problems.

***Handling:*** Keep handling to a minimum, particularly in the first few days of acclimatization. Before touching your Uromastyx regularly, let it become used to its surroundings. To lessen stress, provide your lizard with enough body support while handling it.

***Environmental Enrichment:*** To make your Uromastyx feel safe, provide them places to hide and climb inside the cage. You may create hides out of rocks, plants, or faux reptile décor from a store.

***Avoiding Overcrowding:*** If you have more than one Uromastyx, make sure they have adequate room to prevent fighting over territory, which may cause tension.

## Final Thoughts

A comprehensive strategy that includes appropriate environmental conditions, diet, routine health exams, veterinarian treatment, and stress management is needed to maintain your Uromastyx's health and welfare. You may contribute to the long and healthy life of your Uromastyx by taking proactive measures in its care. Being a caring and attentive owner and strengthening the link you have with your pet ultimately depend on your ability to understand the requirements of these interesting reptiles.

## *CHAPTER 9:*

# UROMASTYX BREEDING AND REPRODUCTION

### *Introduction to Uromastyx Breeding*

For committed aficionados, raising Uromastyx may be a pleasant experience, but it does involve careful preparation, an awareness of their reproductive habits, and knowledge of how to properly care for both the adults and the hatchlings. The fundamentals of breeding Uromastyx will be covered in this chapter, including choosing breeding partners, comprehending their mating habits, setting up ideal mating habitats, and tending to eggs and hatchlings.

## 1. Picking Couples for Breeding

The selection of healthy breeding partners is the first stage in the breeding of Uromastyx. The following are the crucial things to think about:

*Health:* Make sure the male and female Uromastyx are disease-free and in good health. Prior to breeding, a veterinarian examination might assist in determining any underlying health concerns.

*Age:* Uromastyx usually attain sexual maturity between the ages of 1.5 and 2. At this age,

breeding individuals should be able to withstand the physical demands of reproduction.

*Genetic variety:* It is recommended to breed Uromastyx from several bloodlines in order to increase genetic variety and lower the danger of hereditary illnesses. Steer clear of inbreeding, since this may result in kids with health issues.

## 2. Gaining Knowledge about Breeding Behavior

Understanding Uromastyx breeding habits and readiness signals is essential prior to breeding:

*courting:* Head bobbing, tail waving, and chasing are examples of courting activities shown by uromastyx. In an attempt to attract ladies, men often project authority by aggressive posture.

*Mating:* The mating process, which may take many hours, starts as soon as the female is receptive. The male will mount the female during this period, and conception occurs.

*Indications of Pregnancy:* About 30 days after mating, female uromastyx may show indications of pregnancy. Keep an eye out for any changes in behavior, including a rise in hunger or nest-building habits. Another sign that eggs are growing might be a visible bulge in the belly.

### 3. Establishing a Proper Environment for Breeding

A suitable setting is necessary for productive reproduction. Here's how to prepare your enclosure for breeding:

***Enclosure Size:*** In order to accommodate the breeding couple and provide them freedom of movement, a bigger enclosure is required. For a breeding pair, a minimum size of 40 gallons is advised.

***Humidity and Temperature:*** Keep the temperature gradients acceptable, with a colder region about 75°F to 85°F (24°C - 29°C) and a basking area between 100°F and 120°F (38°C - 49°C). Maintain low humidity, preferably in the range of 20% to 40%.

***Nest Box:*** Set up a special nesting space or box that is filled with an appropriate substrate, such soil mixed with sand. This will incentivize the female to deposit her eggs in a secure and cozy setting.

## 4. Incubation and Laying of Eggs

If the female is genuinely gravid after a successful mating, she will deposit eggs. It is essential to comprehend how eggs are laid and how to properly incubate them.

***Laying Eggs:*** Depending on the species and individual, uromastyx usually lay anywhere from six to twenty eggs. To build a nest and deposit her eggs, the female will excavate a hole in the substrate.

***Incubation Conditions:*** It's critical to provide the eggs the correct care once they are deposited.

Gently move the eggs to a separate habitat with regulated humidity and temperature, or an incubator. For optimal results, incubation temperatures of 82°F to 88°F (28°C to 31°C) with relative humidity levels of 60% are recommended for Uromastyx eggs.

***Duration of Incubation:*** Depending on the species and temperature, uromastyx eggs may hatch in 60 to 90 days. Regularly examine the eggs for symptoms of mold or degradation.

### 5. Taking Care of Hatchlings

The survival and growth of the hatchlings depends on providing them with the right care once the eggs hatch.

***Configuring Hatchling Enclosure:*** Move the hatchlings to an enclosure apart from their parents that is the same temperature and humidity. To give them a sense of security and to provide hiding places, the enclosure should be smaller.

***Feeding:*** To support their fast development, hatchlings need a meal high in nutrients. Present a selection of leafy greens that have been finely cut and commercial Uromastyx diets. Make sure they always have access to fresh water.

***Growth Monitoring:*** Keep a regular eye on the hatchlings' development and well-being. Make sure they are eating well and exercising in a healthy way.

### 6. Obstacles in Uromastyx Breeding

Raising Uromastyx might provide some difficulties. Typical problems include the following:

*Infertility:* Not every pairing produces viable eggs or successful fertilization. A female's failure to produce eggs might be a sign of illness or unfavorable circumstances.

*Egg Incubation Issues:* Inadequate humidity or temperature may cause eggs to die or hatchlings to be malformed. Always try to provide the best circumstances possible for incubation.

*Hatchling Care:* Some hatchlings may be weaker than others and need special care. Be ready to help those who have difficulty thriving.

### *Final Thoughts*

Careful preparation, familiarity with the reproductive habits of Uromastyx, and a dedication to giving the adults and hatchlings the finest care possible are all necessary for successful breeding. You may successfully breed Uromastyx and aid in the captive breeding of these unusual lizards if you have the proper conditions, keep an eye on your health, and put in a lot of effort.

## *CHAPTER 10:*

# UROMASTYX MAINTENANCE AND CARE

### *Overview of Uromastyx Treatment*

Uromastyx need a stable habitat, a healthy diet, frequent checkups, and an awareness of their behavioral requirements in order to be properly cared for. A thorough approach to care will guarantee the long-term health and happiness of your Uromastyx. The many facets of caring for and maintaining Uromastyx will be covered in this chapter, with particular attention paid to habitat construction, food needs, handling and socializing, and general health management.

## 1. Establishing and Maintaining a Habitat

An appropriate environment must be created and kept up for your Uromastyx to be healthy.

Size and Type of Enclosure: Uromastyx need a roomy enclosure in order to flourish. For an adult alone, a minimum capacity of 40 gallons is advised; greater quantities work well for couples or gatherings. As long as they have enough ventilation, glass terrariums, wooden enclosures, or plastic containers may all function.

**Substrate Selections:** Select a substrate that minimizes the possibility of impaction while permitting natural digging activities. Paper towels, sand-soil mixtures, and ceramic tiles are safe choices. Steer clear of ingestible loose materials like sand.

***Illuminations and Heating:*** UVB illumination and appropriate heating are essential. A hot area between 100°F and 120°F (38°C and 49°C) may be created by installing a basking lamp. The colder side of the cage should stay between 75°F and 85°F (24°C and 29°C). To provide the UV light required for calcium metabolism, use a UVB bulb and change it every six months.

***Humidity Control:*** Humidities between 20% and 40% are ideal for uromastyx growth. Use a hygrometer to keep an eye on the humidity levels, and make sure there is enough ventilation to avoid moisture accumulation.

## 2. Nutritional Needs

A balanced diet is essential for your Uromastyx Is general health and wellbeing.

***Basic Diet Composition:*** As a herbivorous species, uromastyx do best on a diet high in leafy greens, vegetables, and some fruits. Mustard, dandelion, and collard greens are among the suggested greens. Additionally, you may include an assortment of veggies, such as squash and bell peppers.

***Supplementation:*** Give calcium and vitamin supplements to guarantee optimum health. Once a week, dust their food with powdered calcium and give them a weekly multivitamin.

*Hydration:* Although Uromastyx don't need a lot of water, fresh water must be given to them on a regular basis. They can stay more hydrated by using a shallow water dish and sometimes sprinkling their food.

### 3. Managing and Introducing

Being able to manage and interact with your Uromastyx appropriately is crucial for fostering trust and lowering anxiety.

*Handling Techniques:* Always support your Uromastyx's body while handling it to prevent damage. Allow the lizard to adjust to your presence before trying to handle it routinely. Start out with brief handling sessions and as your Uromastyx becomes more comfortable, gradually extend them.

*Socialization:* Although uromastyx may be gregarious creatures, encounters with people need to be handled with caution. If you want your Uromastyx to become used to your presence without any direct handling, spend some time around the cage.

*symptoms of Stress:* Be alert for any symptoms of stress, such as twitching of the tail, fast breathing, or efforts to flee. If your Uromastyx exhibits signs of stress, put it back in its cage right away.

### 4. Frequent Medical Exams

Regular physical examinations are crucial for the early identification of health problems.

***Visual Inspections:*** Keep an eye out for healthy signals from your Uromastyx on a regular basis. Examine for unbroken skin, healthy eyes, and regular fecal production. A well-nourished Uromastyx should be awake, energetic, and have a good appetite.

***Weight Monitoring:*** To keep tabs on the condition of your Uromastyx, weigh it often. Unexpected weight fluctuations may be a sign of underlying medical conditions that need to be addressed.

Veterinary Care: Find a veterinarian who specializes in reptiles and build a rapport with them. Your Uromastyx may be monitored with routine examinations wellbeing and take care of any issues.

## 5. Identifying Typical Health Problems

Proactively managing the health of your Uromastyx requires awareness of possible health risks.

***Bone Metabolic Disorder (MBD):*** MBD, a prevalent ailment in reptiles, is brought on by deficiency in calcium and ultraviolet B radiation. Make sure your Uromastyx receives the right amount of calcium supplements and UVB illumination.

***Respiratory Infections:*** Lethargy, nasal discharge, and difficult breathing are some of the symptoms. To avoid respiratory problems, keep the temperature and humidity at the right levels.

***Parasites:*** The health of your Uromastyx may be impacted by both internal and external parasites. A veterinarian's routine inspection of the feces may aid in the diagnosis and treatment of parasite illnesses.

## 6. Enhancement of Environment

By providing environmental enrichment, you can maintain the mental well-being and natural habits of your Uromastyx.

***Hiding Spots and Climbing Structures:*** Use logs, rocks, or store-bought reptile décor to create a variety of hiding places. To promote physical exercise, provide climbing possibilities utilizing branches or platforms.

***Different Diets:*** Providing a range of food products not only satisfies dietary requirements but also stimulates the mind. Try a variety of veggies, leafy greens, and sometimes fruits.

## Final Thoughts

Understanding Uromastyx's demands and giving them a secure, stimulating habitat are essential components in caring for them. You can make sure your Uromastyx stays healthy, happy, and a treasured member of your family with the right habitat design, nutrition management, routine health checks, and knowledge of their behavioral needs. Fostering a meaningful relationship with your Uromastyx may be achieved by taking a proactive approach to their care.

## *CHAPTER 11:*

# UROMASTYX OWNERSHIP: ETHICAL CONSIDERATIONS

### *Overview of Ethical Obligation*

Taking care of an Uromastyx requires more than just giving it food and shelter. It means recognizing and meeting the special requirements of these reptiles, encouraging their welfare, and making sure that the care they get complies with moral principles. The ethical aspects of owning a uromastyx are covered in this chapter, with a focus on responsible pet ownership, environmental concerns, and the value of education.

## *1. Adopting Puppies Responsibly*

***Commitment:*** Since uromastyx may live up to 20 years or more in captivity, owning one requires a long-term dedication. Prospective owners must to think about their ability to provide the animal the care it needs for the duration of its life.

***Research:*** It's important to learn all there is to know about the needs, habits, and habitat requirements of Uromastyx before obtaining one. Knowing what they require in particular helps you to give the right atmosphere and food.

***Informed choice:*** Considering the responsibilities involved, buying an Uromastyx should be a well-informed choice. Impulsive purchases often result in subpar care, which may lead to neglect or abandonment.

## 2. Responsible Sourcing of Uromastyx

***Wild Caught vs. Captive Bred:*** If you're purchasing an Uromastyx, go for captive-bred animals instead of wild-caught ones. Captive breeding guarantees that the lizard is accustomed to life in captivity and lessens the strain on wild populations.

***Reputable Breeders:*** Go with respectable breeders that follow moral breeding procedures and give animal welfare first priority. These breeders need to be familiar with the species and able to provide records of the animal's medical background and pedigree.

***Steer Clear of Pet retailers:*** A lot of pet retailers get their animals from mass breeders who could put money above the wellbeing of the animals. Make sure the pet shop has a solid reputation and offers healthy animals before making a purchase.

### 3. Concerns for Welfare

***Environmental Enrichment:*** In order to flourish, uromastyx need an environment that is stimulating. Enriching them with climbing frames, hiding places, and natural behavior chances is crucial for their mental and physical health.

***Health Monitoring:*** It's important to have regular checkups and to keep an eye out for any symptoms of disease or stress. When veterinarian treatment is required, a prudent owner should be prompt in making the appointment.

***Avoiding Impaction:*** If improper substrates are supplied to uromastyx or they are not given enough water, they may have gastrointestinal impaction. Preventing health difficulties may be achieved by giving children appropriate meals and being mindful of their nutritional demands.

## 4. Environmental Concerns

Dangers to Natural Populations: Threats to the native habitats of many Uromastyx species include habitat degradation, climate change, and illicit wildlife trading. Understanding these matters is essential to ethical ownership.

***Encouraging Conservation:*** Owners may support conservation efforts by advocating for the maintenance of their Uromastyx and by responsibly owning them. Encourage the work of groups devoted to the protection of reptiles and spread the word about the value of protecting natural environments.

***Avoid illicit Trade:*** Buying Uromastyx from dubious sources might support the illicit wildlife trade, endangering natural population levels. Before making a purchase, be sure the animal is legal and comes from an ethical source.

### 5. Knowledge and Observation

***Teaching Others:*** You may have a significant impact on teaching others about safe reptile keeping if you possess an Uromastyx. Educate the public and other pet owners on the value of conservation, ethical sourcing, and good pet care.

***Taking Part in Community Events:*** Attend regional pet fairs, reptile exhibits, and educational seminars to raise awareness of conservation and care initiatives for Uromastyx. Your participation may encourage others to adopt a moral stance on pet ownership.

***Online Communities:*** Participate in social media groups and online forums devoted to owning Uromastyx. These venues allow opportunities to exchange experiences, learn from others, and encourage responsible behaviors within the community.

## 6. *Extended-Term Dedication and Organization*

Getting Ready for Longevity: Owners of Uromastyx need to make long-term care arrangements since these animals may live for many years. Throughout the lizard's life, this entails providing a steady living environment, regular feeding, and continuous health monitoring.

***Considerations for Life Changes:*** Owners should have a strategy in place for prospective relocations, family changes, or financial adjustments since life circumstances may change over time. Think about how these things may affect your capacity to take care of your Uromastyx.

***Rehoming Responsibly:*** Please rehome your Uromastyx responsibly if the situation calls for it. To make sure the lizard is housed in a secure setting, find a qualified and informed new owner or get in touch with neighborhood reptile rescue groups.

### Final Thoughts

Understanding uromastyx requirements, encouraging ethical behavior, and supporting conservation efforts are all part of ethical ownership. Owners may guarantee the well-being of their Uromastyx and contribute to the conservation of the species for posterity by emphasizing the welfare of these reptiles and raising awareness and education about them.

## *CHAPTER 12:*

# TAKING PLEASURE IN UROMASTYX: SOCIAL AND CULTURAL ACTIVITIES

### *Overview of Pleasure and Enhancement*

Uromastyx may be interesting companions and provide their owners with special pleasures. Bonding and enrichment activities with your Uromastyx may improve your connection and help your pet's general health. This chapter looks at methods to enjoy your Uromastyx, emphasizing the value of enrichment activities, interactive care, and behavior analysis.

## 1. Developing a Relationship with Your Uromastyx

***Spending Time Together:*** Patience and consistency are needed to develop a connection with your Uromastyx. Give your lizard some time to become used to your presence by spending time around the enclosure. As they get used to handling, progressively introduce it while keeping a calm distance from them.

***Routine Handling:*** Establish a schedule for taking care of your Uromastyx. Your lizard will get more used to human contact with brief, frequent sessions. It should always be handled softly, with its body supported, and without abrupt movements that might frighten it.

***Positive Reinforcement:*** Foster trust by using positive reinforcement. Treats like little bits of lush greens may be given when your Uromastyx comes over. This may foster a favorable perception of your presence.

### 2. Activities to Enhance Uromastyx

***Exploration Opportunities:*** Provide a secure, supervised setting for your Uromastyx to explore outside of its cage. Establish a space under monitoring with safe surfaces. This may encourage instinctive exploring habits.

***Interactive Toys:*** Giving Uromastyx something to explore may be enriching, even if they might not play with toys in the same manner as dogs or cats. Provide branches, pebbles, or cardboard boxes so people may hide and climb them.

***Obstacle Courses:*** Using natural, safe materials, construct basic obstacle courses. Encourage your Uromastyx to climb, study, and explore as you lead it through the course. Engaging in this pastime offers both mental and physical stimulation.

### 3. Eating a Diet Can Be Fun

***Feeding Enrichment:*** Vary the way food is presented to make mealtimes an engaging experience. To promote foraging behavior, distribute food around the cage or conceal it in cracks rather than putting it in a dish.

***Diversity in Diet:*** You may add excitement to feeding time by providing a range of greens, veggies, and even sweets. Try a variety of meals and discover what your Uromastyx likes, but be sure to keep it healthy and balanced.

Hand feeding is something that some Uromastyx may find enjoyable. This makes it possible to communicate directly, fosters trust, and makes feeding times enjoyable.

### 4. Getting Along with Other Animals

***Cautionary Introduction:*** Socializing your Uromastyx with other pets may be beneficial, but it has to be done with caution if you have other pets. Oversee every encounter to avoid tension or injury. Some owners find success with quiet, non-predatory pets or under supervision from other reptiles.

***Understanding Body Language:*** Pay attention to your Uromastyx's nonverbal cues while interacting with them. In order to prevent unpleasant encounters, signs of tension or pain should induce a quick separation.

### 5. Occasion-Based Events

outside Exploration: Think about giving your Uromastyx some supervised outside time during the summer months. Its health and happiness may be enhanced by natural sunshine and fresh air found in a safe, enclosed outside area. To avoid overheating, keep an eye on the temperature.

***Seasonal Enrichment:*** Change out the enrichment materials in the enclosure of your Uromastyx on a seasonal basis. Modify the arrangement or add fresh hiding places, climbing frames, or organic accents. This keeps things interesting and stops people from becoming bored.

## 6. *Seeing Your Uromastyx and Gaining Knowledge from It*

***Behavioral Observation:*** Pay attention to the habits and inclinations of your Uromastyx. You may improve its quality of life by customizing your interactions and enrichment activities based on your understanding of its preferences.

***Growing from Relationships:*** Every Uromastyx is an individual. Observe how it responds to various stimuli and modify your approach according to how comfortable it is with you.

This will strengthen your relationship and enhance the care you provide.

## Final Thoughts

Creating a loving atmosphere that encourages engagement and enrichment is essential to enjoying your uromastyx. You may improve your connection and your Uromastyx's general well-being by getting to know your lizard, giving it engaging activities, and being aware of its requirements. Interacting with your Uromastyx not only makes you happy but also guarantees your pet's happiness and health, which enhances your time spent with them.

## CHAPTER 13:

# FREQUENTLY ASKED QUESTION AND ANSWERS (FAQS)

Common Questions (FAQs) Concerning House Pet Uromastyx

### 1. What is an Uromastyx, and why is it an excellent pet?

*Reaction:* The genus Uromastyx, often called spiny-tailed lizards, is mostly distributed in Africa and the Middle East. They are popular as pets because of their unusual look, relatively minimal maintenance needs, and typically placid demeanor. Because uromastyx are available in a variety of varieties, each with unique colors and sizes, they appeal to reptile lovers. They are popular for being curious and have the ability to form strong bonds with their owners, which makes them wonderful companions.

## 2. What sort of environment is required for Uromastyx?

**Reaction:** Uromastyx need a large cage that reflects the dry, natural habitat in which they live. Smaller species can get by with a 40-gallon tank, while bigger species could need a 75-gallon tank or more. The environment need to comprise:

*Heating:* A warm spot to bask with an approximate temperature of 100° to 120°F, and a somewhat colder side between 75° and 85°F.

- *Lighting:* Because full-spectrum UVB illumination promotes general wellbeing and aids in calcium absorption, it is vital to their health.

- *Substrate:* To encourage natural digging activity, choose a safe substrate like sand or coconut coir. Steer clear of loose substrates since they may cause impaction.

- *Hiding Spots:* To assist lower stress levels, provide a variety of hiding places, such as caves, rocks, or commercial reptile décor.


## 3. What is consumed by Uromastyx?

*Reaction:* Primarily herbivorous, uromastyx flourish when fed fresh greens, vegetables, and sometimes fruits. What they ought to eat is:

*Greens:* kale, mustard greens, dandelion greens, and collard greens.

- *Vegetables:* bell peppers, carrots, and squash.

- *Fruits:* Serve little portions of fruits as snacks, such as papaya, mango, and berries.

- *Calcium Supplement:* To avoid metabolic bone disease, sprinkle a calcium supplement over their meals several times a week.

Make sure their food is diverse enough to provide all the nutrients they need.

### 4. When should I feed my Uromastyx?

*Reaction:* Juveniles Uromastyx need to be fed more frequently—roughly every day—while adults should only be fed two to three times each week. Keep an eye on their weight and change the frequency of feedings as needed. It is vital to serve fresh meals everyday and eliminate any uneaten food to avoid mold and bacteria development.

### 5. *Is Uromastyx manageable, and if so, how should I address it safely?*

***Reaction:*** It is possible to manage uromastyx, but it is important to do so softly and considerately of their comfort level. To ensure safe handling, heed this advice:

**- *Approach Slowly:*** To prevent frightening your Uromastyx, always approach it in a composed manner.

- Support Their Body: When raising someone, support their body with both hands. Refrain from catching them by the tail as this may injure or stress them.

***Limit Handling Time:*** Whenever your Uromastyx is acclimating to a new environment, try to keep handling sessions brief.

You may progressively extend the amount of time you spend engaging with your Uromastyx as they become used to being handled.

### 6. *What medical conditions are prevalent in Uromastyx?*

***Reaction:*** In Uromastyx, common health problems include:

- ***Metabolic Bone Disease (MBD):*** UVB radiation and low calcium levels are the causes of MBD.

- ***Respiratory Infections:*** Usually brought on by improper humidity or temperature, symptoms include difficulty breathing and nasal discharge.

- ***Gastrointestinal Impaction:*** This may be brought on by consuming the wrong kinds of substrates or dehydration.

- ***Parasites:*** They may be impacted by both internal and external parasites.

Frequent veterinarian examinations and keeping an eye out for any symptoms of disease may aid in quickly addressing these problems.

### 7. How can I provide my Uromastyx with a stimulating environment?

***Reaction:*** Take into account the following while creating a stimulating atmosphere for your Uromastyx:

- Hiding Spots: Create hiding places with logs, rocks, and faux reptile décor.

Climbing Frameworks: Encourage climbing and exploring by using branches and platforms.

- Varied Diet: To encourage foraging activity, provide a range of meals and disperse them across the cage.

- Modify the Design: Rearranging the environment from time to time will help to keep your Uromastyx active and avoid boredom.

These improvements will support the continued mental and physical stimulation of your Uromastyx.

**8. *What is the optimal temperature and humidity range for Uromastyx?***

***Reaction:*** Uromastyx need distinct temperature gradients in their habitat:

***Swimming Area:*** between 100°F and 120°F.
***Cold Side:*** between 75°F and 85°F.
- ***Twilight Temperature:*** May decrease to a range of 70° to 75°F.

Relatively low humidity levels, between 30% and 40%, are ideal to replicate their native dry habitat. Make sure the enclosure has enough airflow and use a hygrometer to keep an eye on the humidity levels.

**9. *Are novices able to use Uromastyx?***

*Reaction:* For novices, particularly those who are prepared to dedicate themselves to learning about their care needs, uromastyx may be a good option. Despite their unique dietary, environmental, and thermal requirements, their typically calm disposition makes them easy to handle even for inexperienced reptile caretakers. But it's important to do your homework and be ready for the long-term commitment that comes with owning a uromastyx.

## 10. How can I determine if my Uromastyx is sick or under stress?

*Reaction:* Indications of tension or disease in the ureomastyx might be:

- *Behavioral Changes:* Aggression, sluggishness, or excessive hiding.

*- Physical Symptoms:* Changes in appetite, breathing difficulties, swelling, and irregular posture.

Temperature Regulation Issues: Overindulging in warmth or retreating from sources of heat.

To determine the health and wellbeing of your Uromastyx, speak with a veterinarian who has expertise treating reptiles if you see any of these symptoms.

## 11. Am I able to maintain more than one Uromastyx together?

*Reaction:* The territorial habits of numerous Uromastyx might make them difficult to keep together. If you want to have many, make sure that:

- *Ample Space:* There is enough room in the enclosure for each lizard to have its own territory.

- *Watching Interactions:* Keep a watchful eye out for any indications of tension or aggressiveness in their conduct.

*Compatibility:* To lower the likelihood of conflict, only live with people who are comparable in size and disposition.

Be ready to separate them into separate cages if you see any hostility.

## 12. How do I proceed if I am unable to take care of my Uromastyx?

*Reaction:* It's critical to appropriately rehome your Uromastyx if you are unable to care for it. Think about doing these actions:

**- Get in Touch with Your Local Reptile Rescue:**
A lot of groups focus on finding new homes for reptiles and may provide your Uromastyx a secure atmosphere.

**- Make Contact with Other Fans of Reptiles:**
Make connections with other reptile owners who may be thinking in adopting.

**- Avoid Abandonment:** Since Uromastyx are not native to the area and may disturb local ecosystems, you should never abandon them.

Ensuring responsible rehoming guarantees that your Uromastyx keeps getting the attention it needs.

This chapter provides a thorough reference for frequent issues and queries that both existing and potential Uromastyx users may have.

Readers will be better able to make choices about taking care of their Uromastyx and cultivating a fulfilling pet-owner connection if concise, educational responses are provided.

www.ingramcontent.com/pod-product-compliance
Lightning Source LLC
Chambersburg PA
CBHW071023250726
48653CB00005B/1686